Religions Today

Islam

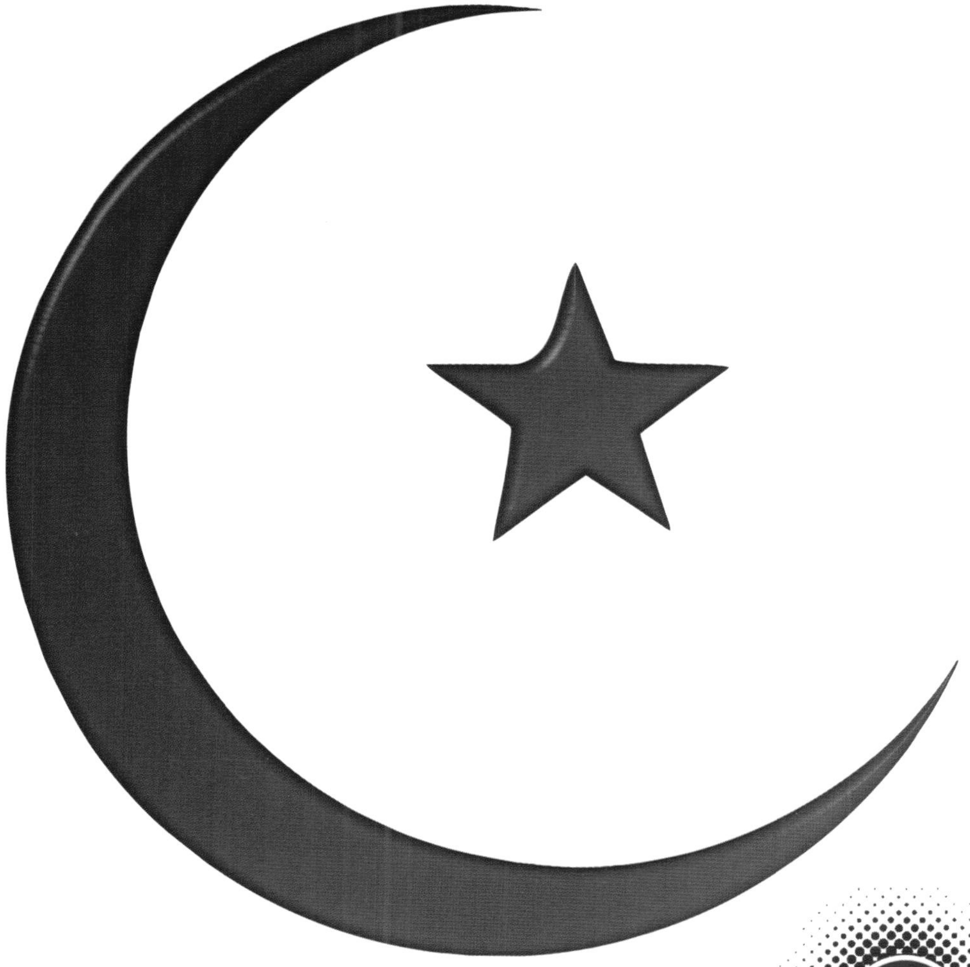

Andrew Egan

Heinemann
LIBRARY

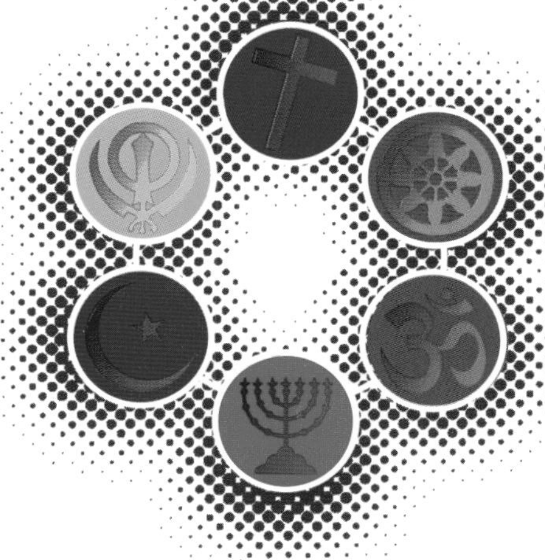

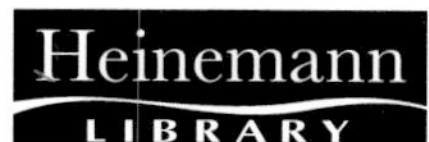

For Olivia

Heinemann Library
Halley Court, Jordan Hill, Oxford, OX2 8EJ
a division of Reed Educational and Professional Publishing Ltd

OXFORD MELBOURNE AUCKLAND
JOHANNESBURG BLANTYRE GABORONE
IBADAN PORTSMOUTH (NH) USA CHICAGO

First published in 2002

ISBN 0 431 14973 9 (hardback)
06 05 04 03 02
10 9 8 7 6 5 4 3 2 1

ISBN 0 431 14980 1 (paperback)
07 06 05 04 03
10 9 8 7 6 5 4 3 2 1

British Library Cataloguing in Publication Data
A catalogue record for this book is available from the British Library

Picture research by Jennifer Johnson
Designed and typeset by Artistix, Thame, Oxon
Printed and bound in Spain by Edelvives

Acknowledgements
The author would like to thank Imam Aurangzeb Khan for all the wise words and kind prayers that have helped to make this book possible.

The publishers would like to thank the following for permission to use photographs:

Andes Press Agency/Carlos Reyes-Mayer, p. 45; Andes Press Agency/D&C Hill, p. 52; Andrew Egan, p. 8; Hutchison Picture Library/Edward Parker, p. 44; Hutchison Picture Library/Nigel Smith, p. 42; Hutchison Picture Library/Titus Moser, p. 15; Panos Pictures/Jeremy Hartley, pp. 47 and 48; Panos Pictures/Penny Tweedie, p. 51; Rex Features/Eastlight Vienna, p. 55; Science Photo Library/Celestial Image Co., p. 57; Science Photo Library/ESA/Photo Library International, p. 40; Science Photo Library/Peter Menzel, p. 56. All other photographs supplied by Peter Sanders.

The publishers have made every effort to contact copyright holders. However, if any material has been incorrectly acknowledged, the publishers would be pleased to correct this at the earliest opportunity.

Contents

An introduction to Islam

In this section you will:

- understand the words faith and trust and their importance to Muslims
- think about the ways in which Islam seeks to strengthen faith in Allah.

Faith and trust

As in all religions **belief** is important in **Islam**. Belief means that you have no doubt, even if sometimes it is hard to back up your belief.

Belief needs **faith** and **trust**. Faith is the courage to accept the challenges to your belief; trust means that you feel sure that you won't be let down.

The people who follow Islam are called **Muslims**. The worldwide community of Muslims is known as the **ummah**. Islam is like one great family – the only difference is local culture and custom.

Allah

All Muslims have faith and trust in **Allah**. Muslims believe that Allah is the Almighty God who created the universe. For Muslims, Islam is more than just a series of beliefs, it is a way of life. Muslims believe Allah has given guidance to help all people live good lives. So to be a true Muslim means to accept Allah as God and to do His will.

Standing before Allah in prayer

Islam teaches that all people are equal. However, the best people are those who are most faithful to Allah.

A Muslim family

The aims of Islam

Islam lets people make up their own minds. Islam wants to free people from sin, so that they can live their lives doing their best in the eyes of Allah. Islam also aims to free human beings from greed, from envy, from fear and from feeling insecure. Islam wants to free people from the worship of false gods, and develop goodness and excellence inside of them. Islam is about obeying completely the will of Allah.

Islam wants to see its followers as honest and kind-hearted, reliable and sincere. Muslims show this through worship and the way in which they treat other people.

Muslims know that their faith is true because they believe Allah has told people about Himself over the years. He has done this through holy people known as **prophets**. The **Qur'an**, the Muslim holy book, mentions by name 25 prophets of Allah, beginning with **Adam (pbuh)** and finishing with **Muhammad** (pbuh).

To show respect to the prophets of Islam, Muslims will say 'peace be upon him' when mentioning a prophet by name. Throughout this book (pbuh) will appear as a sign of respect when the names of the prophets are mentioned. For Muslims, the last and greatest of the prophets was Muhammad (pbuh). Allah revealed the Qur'an to Muhammad (pbuh). Muslims believe the Qur'an to be Allah's final message to guide human beings in the ways of true religion.

The importance of faith and trust

Faith and trust are very important parts of life. We trust the equipment in our homes, and the cars and buses we ride on. Also, we trust the people around us. Our families and friends are important to us, but so are doctors, dentists and teachers, and police, fire and rescue services. We trust them all.

Trust is a very important part of life. Without it, we would hardly get anything done because we would spend all our time doubting and questioning everything.

The only things that can be seen as reliable are things such as 2 + 2 = 4. This is a fact and is always right. However, such a fact is of no use to you if you need to see the dentist or receive first aid. It is experience that informs most of our judgements. If we have a good experience of something or someone, then we are most likely to trust it or them.

It is in this way that Muslims trust Allah and have faith in Him. Their experience of the world that Allah has made helps Muslims to trust that Allah is a God of power and love.

The prophet Muhammad (pbuh)

In this section you will:

- find out about the prophet Muhammad (pbuh)
- begin to understand the message Muhammad (pbuh) was to give to the people of Makkah
- read about Muhammad's (pbuh) calling.

Muhammad's (pbuh) childhood

Muhammad (**pbuh**) was born in Makkah in 569 CE. **Makkah** is now in the modern country of Saudi Arabia. By the time Muhammad was eight, his parents and grandparents were dead. He went to live with his uncle, **Abu Talib**.

The prophet of Islam

The people of Makkah didn't understand who **Allah** was. They put their **faith** in statues and lucky charms and hoped that they would help them. Muhammad (pbuh) was not like the others, he was a man of faith and prayed regularly.

Muhammad (pbuh) would pray in the hills outside Makkah. Muhammad's (pbuh) faith grew stronger and stronger. He would often sit by himself in a cave on **Jabal-un-Nur** (the Mountain of Light). He would pray and share his food with passers-by.

When he was 40 years old Muhammad (pbuh) was praying one night when the **Angel Jibril** appeared in the cave.

The Angel told him to read out loud the words on the cloth he was carrying. Although he could not read before that night, Muhammad (pbuh) read out loud the following verses:

'In the name of Allah, Most Gracious, Most Merciful.
Recite! (read aloud): In the name of your Lord Who has created;
He has Created man from a clot.
Recite! And your Lord is Most Generous.
Who taught by the pen,
He has taught man that which he knew not.'

Qur'an, **surah** 96: 1–5

Muhammad (pbuh) was amazed by what had happened and went home dazed. He told **Khadijah**, his wife, what had happened to him. Muhammad (pbuh) thought that some evil spirit might be involved. Khadijah said she was sure that Allah would protect him.

Muhammad's (pbuh) marriage to Khadijah was very important as it gave him a firm relationship which would help him do Allah's work. Soon Allah gave Muhammad (pbuh) another message. Allah told Muhammad (pbuh) to warn people against evil and to tell them not to worship any gods except Allah.

'O you enveloped in garments,
Arise and warn!
And magnify your Lord
And purify your garments and keep away from idols.'

Qur'an, surah 74: 1–7

It was important that the people of Makkah heard the will of Allah. They were to change their ways and lead better lives. It was Muhammad's (pbuh) job to make sure this happened.

Allah continued to give Muhammad (pbuh) messages for twenty-three years:

'This day, I have perfected your religion for you and completed My Favour upon you and have chosen for you Islam as your religion.'

Qur'an, surah 5: 3

After Muhammad's (pbuh) death everything that he had received from Allah was written down in the Qur'an, the holy book of **Islam**.

The cave above Makkah

Muhammad's (pbuh) calling

Muslims believe that Muhammad (pbuh) received a calling from Allah. Such a calling is known as a vocation. Muhammad's (pbuh) vocation came as a calling to tell the people of Makkah to change the way they lived. Allah told Muhammad (pbuh) to tell the people that they should stop drinking, swearing and acting violently.

Allah's call to every Muslim

Muslims believe that everyone has the potential to receive a calling from Allah. Not all callings are likely to be as dramatic as the one Muhammad (pbuh) received. But all people do have the potential. For example, Islam teaches that all people have a calling to work hard, whether at school, in a job or around the house.

The exact nature of such callings will vary from person to person. Muslims believe that the most important thing is that everyone is called by Allah in different ways and at different times. It is the basic human duty to respond to Allah's call to the very best of our ability.

The prophets

In this section you will:

- explore the nature of a prophet
- understand and evaluate the importance of prophets for Muslims and read about the prophet 'Isa (Jesus).

The messengers of Allah

Understanding the **prophets** is important for understanding **Islam**. **Muslims** believe that **Muhammad** (**pbuh**) was the last of all the prophets.

The word prophet comes from an Arabic word '**risalah**'. Risalah means 'message'. In this case it means the message to all people to live better lives.

A person can't become a prophet because they want to. It is a special gift that **Allah** gives to a human being. Allah decides who is fit to be a prophet.

In the **Qur'an** this calling from Allah is called **istjfaa**. Istjfaa means choosing the best people. Muslims believe that Allah chose the best people to be prophets. They are people that Allah chose to give special qualities. The prophets were not like other people.

The message

'A prophet never speaks on his own accord
Nor does he speak of (his own) desire. It is only a Revelation revealed (by Allah).'

Qur'an, **surah** 53: 3–4

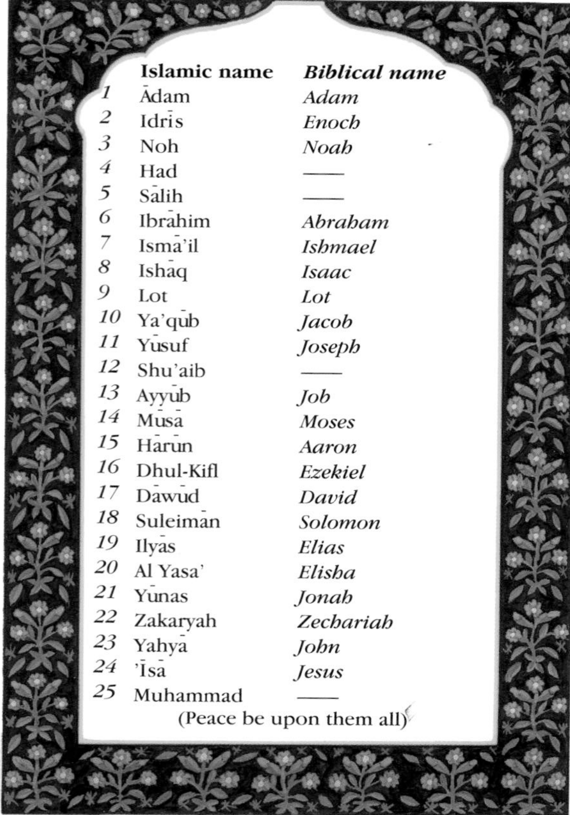

	Islamic name	***Biblical name***
1	Ādam	*Adam*
2	Idrīs	*Enoch*
3	Noh	*Noah*
4	Had	——
5	Sālih	——
6	Ibrāhim	*Abraham*
7	Ismā'il	*Ishmael*
8	Ishāq	*Isaac*
9	Lot	*Lot*
10	Ya'qūb	*Jacob*
11	Yūsuf	*Joseph*
12	Shu'aib	——
13	Ayyūb	*Job*
14	Mūsā	*Moses*
15	Hārūn	*Aaron*
16	Dhul-Kifl	*Ezekiel*
17	Dāwūd	*David*
18	Suleimān	*Solomon*
19	Ilyās	*Elias*
20	Al Yasa'	*Elisha*
21	Yūnas	*Jonah*
22	Zakaryah	*Zechariah*
23	Yahyā	*John*
24	'Īsā	*Jesus*
25	Muhammad	——

(Peace be upon them all)

The prophets of Islam

This means that the prophet cannot change Allah's message. The word of Allah always remains the way Allah wants it to be. It is the fact that Allah has chosen the prophet that makes him different from other human beings. Examples of the teaching of the prophets include:

'He is not a believer who eats his fill while his neighbour remains hungry by his side.'

Muhammad (pbuh)

'There are many who fast during the day and pray all night, but they gain nothing but hunger and sleeplessness.'

Muhammad (pbuh)

'When you fast, wash your face and look happy, that your fasting may not be seen by men but by your Father who is in secret; and your Father who is in secret will reward you.'

'Isa – Jesus (pbuh)

'The Lord is in his holy temple, the Lord's throne is in heaven;...
the Lord is good, he loves good deeds; the upright shall see his face.'

Dawud – David (pbuh)

'The righteous has enough to satisfy his appetite, but the belly of the wicked suffers want.'

Suleiman – Solomon (pbuh)

The commandments from Allah (The Lord – Judaism, God – Christianity) call all people to love and serve both Allah and other people.

Allah's prophets

Muslims believe that over time Allah has sent prophets to tell people something of what He is like. Of all the prophets Muhammad (pbuh) is the most important because he was the last. However, the other prophets are very important, too. Amongst these prophets is 'Isa – Jesus (pbuh).

The prophet 'Isa – Jesus

Christians believe that 'Isa (pbuh) was God's son. They believe that at the end of his life 'Isa was put to death on a cross and, after three days, he came back to life.

Muslims disagree with these beliefs about 'Isa (pbuh). Islam teaches that the birth of 'Isa (pbuh) was a miracle. His mother was the virgin Maryam and he was conceived by the command of Allah (surah 19: 17–21).

Muslims believe that 'Isa (pbuh) became a prophet when he was 30 years old, and that he worked as a prophet for three years (surah 19: 29–34). Allah gave him special powers; he could heal the sick, for example.

Islam says that 'Isa (pbuh) called people to obey Allah alone but that some of his followers considered him to be the son of Allah (surah 5: 116–117). Muslims believe this to be wrong. This is because Allah is one and has no equal.

The Qur'an teaches that prophet 'Isa did not die on a cross. Rather, he was taken up into heaven by Allah.

It is clear that there are many similarities between the Christian and Muslim understanding of prophet 'Isa, but there are many important differences, too.

Muslim leadership and authority

In this section you will:

- learn about the role of the imam in the Muslim community
- consider the important role played by learned people in Islam
- read a selection of Muslim prayers.

The role of the imam

Many religions have local leaders to guide them in their **faith** and to help or comfort them in bad times. For example, Jews have their rabbi and Christians their priest. Jewish rabbis and Christian priests are usually paid for the work they do. This is because the calling to serve God is their full time job. The role of the **imam** in the **Muslim** community is different.

In **Islam** there are generally no paid religious leaders. The **Qur'an** says that Islam should not try to get people to serve **Allah** just because they will be paid.

Imam Aurangzeb Khan

'Leading a community in prayer before Allah is an honour, and teaching the meaning and importance of the word of Allah a privilege; to be paid would add nothing.

'I trained for seven years to become an imam. The training involved full study of both the Qur'an and the **Hadiths**. I felt called to this through a sense of wanting to develop my own prayer life and dedication to Allah.

The honour of being asked to then help others is a great bonus. Allah has given all things, including all our feelings and emotions. One thing in particular that He has given is the ability to ask questions like who am I? where have I come from? and where am I going? in terms of my relationship with Allah. I am a child of Allah and as such I want to grow closer to Him, fully engaged in His service.

'I see my main task as being there to help others to maintain their prayer life. For me my prayer life is rather like owning a car, if you look after it and service it regularly, it will serve you well. So it is with prayer, looked after well your prayer life will flourish and serve you well for life.'

Imam Aurangzeb Khan

The local Muslim community usually chooses the imam. Any Muslim of good character can be an imam providing he:

- has a good knowledge of Islam
- is respected by other Muslims

An imam leading worship in a mosque

- has studied the Qur'an, the holy book of Islam and the Hadiths, the sayings of the prophet **Muhammad** (**pbuh**)
- has deep faith in and love of Allah.

Leading prayers

The main role of the imam is to lead the prayers at the **mosque**. Before the Friday lunchtime prayers, the most important prayers of the week, the imam will give two short talks, called the **khutbah**. These talks will be about the verses of the Qur'an or the Hadiths and their importance for Muslims today.

It is the imam who will often lead the prayers and give a talk at a Muslim marriage or funeral. He will take a leading role in the work of the **madrasah** or school at the mosque where young Muslims will go to study Islam.

The imam, however, is not a leader of Muslims. Islam says that all followers can worship Allah for themselves. The imam is simply a highly respected member of the local community. The imam will try and help everyone in his community to live his or her life the way Allah would want.

Some Muslim prayers

After leading the community in prayer at the mosque, the imam will often make his own personal prayers to Allah. Sometimes, time will be taken to ask Allah for forgiveness and mercy.

The belief that Allah is a loving God is very powerful. Despite being hurt by human sin, Muslims believe that Allah will always grant forgiveness.

As Imam Aurangzeb Khan says, 'In fact there is no real need to say such prayers out loud. Allah knows all the secrets of every heart and so will have forgiven the person who is truly sorry even before they voice their prayer.'

Such prayers can be said either in Arabic (the language of the Qur'an) or in the person's own language.

'O our Lord, grant us good in this world and good in the next world, save us from the punishment of hell.'

'O Allah, you are the source of peace and from you comes peace, you are most highly exalted, O lord of majesty and honour.'

'O Allah, forgive me and my parents and my teachers and all believing men and women and all Muslim men and women in your great mercy. O most merciful lord, you have all mercy.'

Muslim beliefs

In this section you will:
- find out about the most important Muslim beliefs
- read about the pillars of Islam.

Muslims believe that **Islam** is the true religion of **Allah**, the one true God. The most basic **beliefs** of Islam are:

1. in Allah
2. in the will of Allah (predestination)
3. in the **angels** of Allah
4. in the books of Allah
5. in the messengers (**prophets**) of Allah
6. in the day of judgement
7. in life after death.

These seven basic beliefs can be put into three broader groups:

1. **tawhid** – that Allah is God alone, he is like nothing and nothing is like him
2. **risalah** – the work and message of the prophets
3. **akhirah** – life after death.

Tawhid, risalah and akhirah sum up the whole of the Muslim way of life.

Tawhid

Tawhid means that Allah is God. It is the main part of the **faith** of Muslims and is written in the **Qur'an**:

'Say, He is Allah, the One. Allah is the self sufficient master Whom all creatures need. He begets not nor was begotten. And there is none co-equal or comparable to Him.'

Qur'an, **surah** 112

Tawhid means that Allah created everything. It is Allah who is therefore the sustainer of the universe and the only source of human guidance.

'It is Allah alone who has created all things, given all things, is all things. We would have nothing, be nothing without Allah.'

Mariah, aged 14

Risalah

Risalah explains the important role played by the prophets in Islam.

The basic Muslim beliefs

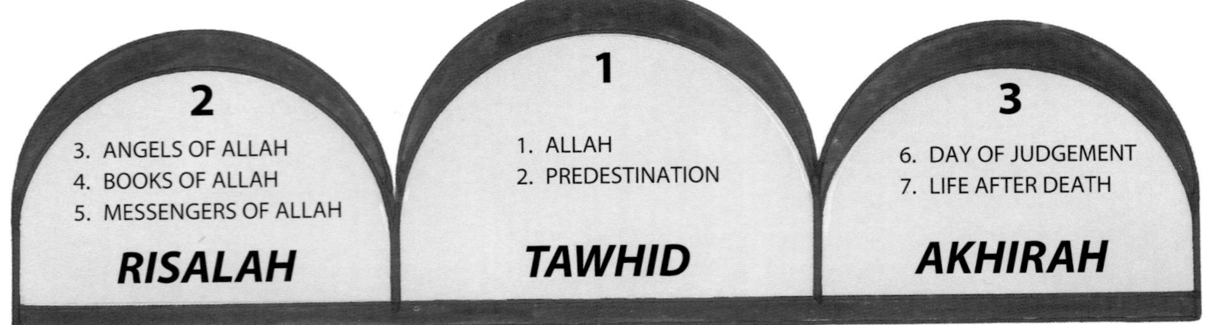

'Allah sent among them a messenger from among themselves, reciting unto them His Verses, and purifying them, and instructing them in the book and wisdom.'

Qur'an, surah 3: 164

This means that:

'Allah has sent His messenger with … the religion of truth, to make it victorious.'

Qur'an, surah 61: 9

'Allah wants to guide us when we go wrong or help us when we misunderstand. For me, the prophets are those specially chosen by Allah to guide and help us to know Allah better and to understand what Allah wants.'

Mudassir, aged 15

Akhirah

Akhirah explains the Muslim belief in life after death. Allah's message is:

'Did you think that We had created you in play and that you would not be brought back to us?'

Qur'an, surah 23: 115

'And those who disbelieve say "when we have become dust we and our fathers, shall we really be brought forth again?"'

Qur'an, surah 27: 67

Muslims believe in life after death because Allah has promised a wonderful afterlife for everyone who believes in him. Allah never breaks His promises.

Islam teaches that human life is one eternal life. Eternal life is made up of two parts: life before and life after death. Muslims believe that in the afterlife Allah will judge all people. It is said that those who have led good lives on earth will enter heaven with Allah. Those who have led bad and wicked lives will be punished.

The pillars of Islam

It is simple to sum up the most basic Muslim beliefs: Allah alone is God and Allah alone is to be worshipped. There are five important parts to Muslim worship, known as the pillars of Islam.

The first pillar is **shahadah**. Shahadah is what every Muslim believes: that there is only one God – Allah – and that **Muhammad** (**pbuh**) is His prophet.

The second pillar is **salah**. Salah means prayer five times a day.

The third pillar is **zakah**. Zakah means giving money to people who are poor or needy.

The fourth pillar is **sawm**. Sawm is fasting (going without food) during the month of **Ramadan**. Fasting helps Muslims to remember Allah and the needs of others.

The fifth pillar is **Hajj**. Hajj is pilgrimage to Makkah. Makkah is the most holy of all places for Muslims.

Allah

In this section you will:

- understand most important characteristics of Allah
- read about and reflect upon how Muslims try to describe Allah.

Muslim beliefs about Allah

Some people seem to pass their entire lives without ever thinking about the reason for their existence. Many think there is a universe and that is all there is. They believe their lives are simply a chain of events until they die.

Muslims, however, say it is impossible for anything to have being or purpose without God. To recognize that **Allah** does exist and is the beginning and end of all things is essential to the **faith** of **Islam**.

Muslims believe that Allah is one and at one with all things and that there is no other god except Him. This **belief** is called **tawhid**. The **prophet Muhammad** (**pbuh**) attacked all forms of belief in God which denied His oneness and unity.

The word 'Islam' means 'submission'. The way in which Muslims submit themselves to the will of Allah reflects what Muslims believe about Allah and the way in which Allah expects them to live.

Allah, the name of God

Shirk

Blasphemy means acting or speaking disrespectfully about God. The Arabic word **shirk** can be understood as describing a form of blasphemy.

Shirk can be thought of as the blasphemy of associating Allah with someone or something else. Anyone who does this commits the most serious blasphemy. The name 'Allah' in Arabic – the language of the **Qur'an** – is singular, and is neither male nor female. Shirk, then, is either the worship of anything other than Allah, or the association of Allah with anything other than Allah.

Why do you think Muslims might feel the power of Allah is displayed in this sunrise?

Understanding Allah

Muslims often find it possible to understand Allah best in terms of the wonders of His creation. The whole universe is Allah's creation and everything in it belongs to Allah and is dependent on Allah.

'Allah alone created all things, gave all things, is all things. Allah is like nothing or no one, Allah is greater than anything we can ever hope to imagine, it's pointless and wrong to ever try to bring Allah down to our level. The love and power of Allah is a beautiful mystery, I'm happy with that.'

Mariah, aged 14

One of the best ways of understanding the power of Allah is by thinking about the light that Allah has provided for the world. The following quotations show how important the gift of light is for Muslims.

'Allah will give you a Light by which you will walk.'

Qur'an, **surah** 57: 28

'O Lord! Illuminate my heart with light, my sight with light and my hearing with light. Let there be light on my right hand and on my left and light behind me and light going before me.'

A prayer of Muhammad (pbuh)

'O God, who knows the innermost secrets of our hearts – lead us out of the darkness into the light.'

A prayer of Muhammad (pbuh)

Names of Allah

Muslims have 99 names for Allah, which describe his varied nature. Here are the first 30 of Allah's names.

God
The Compassionate
The Merciful
The King
The Holy
The Peace
The One with Faith
The Protector
The Mighty
The Repairer
The Imperious
The Creator
The Maker
The Fashioner
The Forgiver
The Dominant
The Bestower
The Provider
The Opener
The Knower
The Contractor
The Expander
The Humbler
The Exalter
The Honourer
The Abaser
The Hearer
The Seer
The Judge
The Just

Thinking about Allah

In this section you will:

- think about why it is not always easy to talk about Allah
- develop an understanding of what Allah is like.

Madrasah: 'Muslim children learning ways to express their beliefs about Allah'

The nature of the universe

For some people, understanding what **Allah** (God) is like is difficult. People have tried to think of Allah as being 'up there', living in a place called Heaven. The opposite can be said for **Shaytan** (the Devil) who lives under the earth in Hell. This might mean that we as human beings live in a sort of middle ground, called earth.

A three-storey depiction of the universe

Science has taught us that the universe in which we live is not like that. We know that Allah does not live in the sky. In fact, the sky, with its many layers, gives protection for the earth from the sun's harmful rays.

We also know that the earth is round, so Hell cannot be below the earth, as that would be sky for people living on the other side of the planet.

The nature of Allah

Muslims talk of Allah as being one total power. The laws of nature and the beauty of creation show just a little of Allah but are not Allah. Allah is greater than the universe, greater than time and space. Allah knows everything and is the all powerful creator and controller of all things.

The beauty of Allah's creation

Muslims often talk of Allah as 'He' or things belonging to Allah as 'His'. This does not mean that Allah is male or that Allah is not female. It just helps human beings, who can only have a little understanding of Allah, to share feelings, prayers and other forms of worship.

The 99 names of Allah

Understanding Allah

Understanding what Allah is like is not easy. This parable, or story, can help us to understand what **faith** in Allah is like.

Two explorers are walking through the jungle when they come to a clearing. Here, many flowers are growing, and also many weeds.

The first explorer says, 'A gardener must tend this spot.' The other disagrees, 'There is no gardener.' So they set up camp and begin watching, but no gardener is ever seen.

'But perhaps he is an invisible gardener,' says the first explorer. So they set up barbed wire, an electric fence and a patrol with bloodhounds. But there are no signs to show that an invisible gardener has visited.

'But,' says the first explorer, 'perhaps there is an invisible gardener, who doesn't feel electric shocks. A gardener who has no scent and makes no sound – a gardener who come secretly to tend the garden he loves.'

'Well,' says the second explorer, 'just how does your invisible gardener differ from a made-up gardener – or, indeed, no gardener at all?'

Muslims would say that there are many things about Allah that are almost impossible to understand. However, it is faith that enable them to look beyond such things, and enjoy the beauty that is at the heart of Allah.

Signs and symbols

In this section you will:

- consider reasons why symbolic language is important
- read about some of the ways Muslims describe Allah in the Qur'an.

Muslims feel little need for symbols in their religion. But to remind them of the way **Allah** guides his people, two very powerful symbols are often used in **Islam**.

The star and crescent moon

Islam began in the desert of Arabia among farmers who would travel by night, away from the heat of the sun. The moon would provide light at night and the stars fixed points by which the people could find their way across the desert. Muslims are happy to think of Allah as the guiding light in their lives. It is Allah who shows them the way to live good lives.

The star and crescent moon are a reminder of the will of **Allah**. They also remind Muslims of the rewards for following Allah.

'Allah is the Spirit, the power behind all things, Allah is in all things, Allah is all things.'

Salim, aged 13

'I know that Allah loves all that He has made. Best of all Allah loves us so we return love in worship.'

Mariah, aged 14

'Allah is every mystery and every answer in the universe.'

Mudassir, aged 15

Religious language

Symbolic language is important in religion. We expect our language to cover a wide range of different jobs. We only have a limited vocabulary and so use the same word for different meanings. For example, the word 'love':

a Olivia loves strawberries

b Olivia loves her Mum and Dad

c Olivia loves her cuddly teddy bear.

A word as popular as love can mean different things to different people at different times.

When people want to talk about God, they have to use the same words that are used in everyday language. So there is a problem in what is meant exactly by saying 'God is good' or 'God loves us'. Two possible answers to this problem might be to say that:

1. **a** religious language is special because it describes something unique

   b religious language is used in special ways and should not be mixed up with language that we use everyday

2. it is because of these difficulties that:

   a symbols – pictures with a powerful meaning

   b analogies, 'symbolic pictures' – for example 'Allah's love for us is like the love of a parent for their child'

   c myths – stories which share with the reader important messages

   are used by people of many religions to talk about their beliefs about God.

Allah in the Qur'an

Here are a selection of analogies, or symbolic pictures, used to describe Allah in the **Qur'an**.

The Mighty
The Forgiving
The Grateful
The Lofty
The Great
The Guardian
The Nourisher
The Light
The Guide
The Gatherer
The Hidden
The First
The Last
The Truth
The Strong
The One
The Loving
The Wise

Decoration in Islam

Muslims have developed a beautiful style of art to decorate **mosques** and editions of the Qur'an, using a variety of designs and patterns. Here is an example of this type of decoration.

Part of surah 112 of the Qur'an

Worship – Shahadah

In this section you will:

- learn about the importance of worshipping Allah for every Muslim
- understand the importance of shahadah in the worship of Allah
- read the words of the adhan.

The most important duty of every **Muslim** is to worship **Allah**. The word 'worship' in English comes from an old word meaning 'to give worth'. Muslims believe that Allah is 'worth' a great deal of praise.

Worshipping Allah means that every Muslim must obey his commands and do his will. The Arabic word for obeying Allah is **ibadah**. Ibadah comes from the Arabic word **abd**, which means servant or slave. A servant or slave obeys their master. Every Muslim would be happy to say that Allah is their master.

There are five duties that are most important in Muslim worship. These five duties, often called 'pillars', include:

1. **shahadah** – a statement of belief in Allah
2. **salah** – prayer five times each day
3. **zakah** – the giving of alms (money) for the poor
4. **sawm** – fasting during the month of **Ramadan**
5. **Hajj** – pilgrimage to **Makkah** at least once in a lifetime

The five pillars of Islam

Shahadah

The first and most important duty of every Muslim is to state their faith in Allah. Islam teaches that a person must speak of their faith in Allah with their lips and believe it in their heart:

'Ash hadu an laa ilaha il-allahu wa Ash hada anna Muhammadar abduhu wa rasulu.'
(I believe there is no god but Allah; and I believe that **Muhammad** (**pbuh**) is the servant and messenger of Allah.)

Saying these Arabic words is called shahadah, the statement of faith. The shahadah is said by Muslims at least twice every day, when they wake up and just before sleeping. The words of the shahadah make up an important part of the Muslim call to prayer (the **adhan**). The adhan is used to call Muslims to prayer five times each day. The call to prayer is also the first words whispered into the ear of a newborn baby. Also, if possible, the last words spoken by a Muslim before they die should be the **Kalimah Tayyibah**. The Kalimah Tayyibah, like the call to prayer, sums up the Muslim belief that Allah is one and that **Muhammad** (**pbuh**) is his servant and messenger.

'The message of **Islam** is very important and very simple, because if Allah wants you to do something he lets you know. The **Prophet** has taught that Allah wants worship, our way of thanking him for everything. This worship is in the five pillars. You make a choice, to follow and worship Allah or not. It's a way of choosing either Heaven (being with Allah) or Hell (being separated from Allah)

'Islam means to submit yourself, give in to Allah. Worshipping Allah involves time and commitment throughout your life. It is right to worship, look at everything we have been given by Allah.'

Shamira, aged 13

The adhan

Islam encourages Muslims to say their compulsory prayers in the **mosque** whenever possible. To call Muslims to prayer, the prophet Muhammad (pbuh) introduced the adhan – the call to prayer. The person who recites the adhan is called the Mu'adhin. He stands in the minaret of the mosque, faces Makkah, raises his hands to his ears and calls out a special form of words.

The words of the adhan

Allahu Akbar
Allahu Akbar
Allahu Akbar
Allahu Akbar
Ash hadu an laa ilaha il-allahu
Ash hadu an laa ilaha il-allahu
Ash hada anna Muhammadar abduhu wa rasulu
Ash hada anna Muhammadar abduhu wa rasulu
Hayya 'alas salah
Hayya 'alas salah
Hayya 'alal falah
Hayya 'alal falah
Allahu Akbar
Allahu Akbar
laa ilaha il-allahu

This may be translated as:

Allah is the greatest
Allah is the greatest
Allah is the greatest
Allah is the greatest
I bear witness that there is no god but Allah
I bear witness that there is no god but Allah
I bear witness that Muhammad is Allah's messenger
I bear witness that Muhammad is Allah's messenger
Rush to prayer
Rush to prayer
Rush to success
Rush to success
Allah is the greatest
Allah is the greatest
There is no god but Allah

Worship – Salah 1

In this section you will:

- understand the importance of prayer
- think about the ways in which Muslims believe prayer can bring individuals closer to Allah
- consider ways in which Muslims pray.

Salah

Salah is one of the five basic duties of **Islam**. Salah means prayer five times every day. The times at which prayers are said are laid down in the **Qur'an**. **Muslims** can come closer to **Allah** by praying regularly, correctly and with a full understanding of its importance and meaning.

Muslims believe that the purpose of human life is to worship Allah. Allah has made this clear in the Qur'an:

'And I created not … mankind except that they worship me.'

Qur'an, **surah** 51: 56

Therefore, Muslims believe that whatever they do, they must remember that they are doing it for Allah.

Muslims at prayer

'Salah is important for a number of reasons:

- it brings men and women closer to Allah
- it is designed to control evil desires and passions
- it purifies the heart, develops the mind and comforts the soul
- it is a constant reminder of Allah and His greatness
- it develops discipline and will power
- it shows that Islam is one universal family – the **ummah**
- it is a means of cleanliness, purity and punctuality
- it is a sign of total obedience to the will of Allah.

The Qur'an teaches that if your prayer life does not improve the way in which you conduct your life, you must think seriously and find out where you are going wrong.'

Imam Aurangzeb Khan

The times of salah

Salah is performed five times every day at special times:

1. Salat-ul-Fajr – between first light and sunrise
2. Salat-ul-Zuhr – just after the sun has left its highest point in the sky
3. Salat-ul-Asr – between mid-afternoon and sunset
4. Salat-ul-Maghrib – between sunset and darkness
5. Salat-ul-Isha – between darkness and dawn.

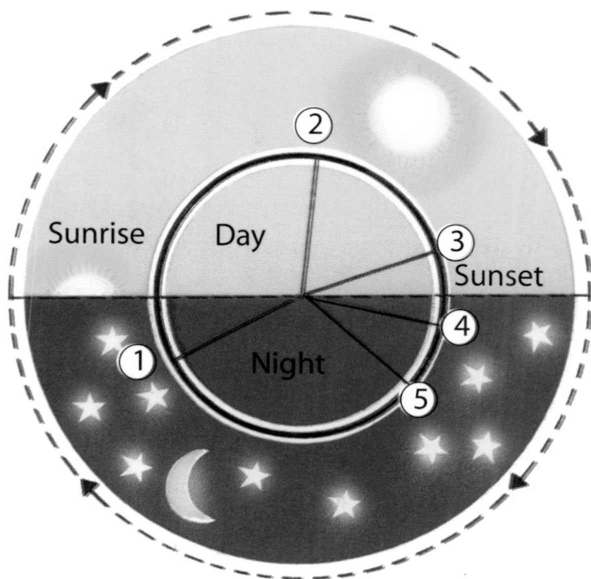

Salah takes place five times a day, at the times shown in this diagram

Rak'ahs

Salah is performed by repeating set movements and prayers. A **rak'ah** is a sequence of set movements.

Two rak'ahs are repeated at Salat-ul-Fajr; four at Salat-ul-Zuhr and Salat-ul-Asr; three at Salat-ul-Maghrib; and four at Salat-ul-Isha. At each rak'ah, set prayers are repeated.

Eight positions make up a rak'ah:

1. standing up straight
2. raising your hands to your ears
3. placing your right hand on your left hand just below your navel or on your chest
4. bowing down
5. placing your hands on your knees
6. prostrating yourself with your forehead, nose, palms of your hands and knees touching the floor
7. kneeling upright
8. whilst still kneeling, turning your face from left to right.

Worship – Salah 2

In this section you will:

- examine the preparations for prayer
- think about the importance of focusing the heart and mind before praying.

Preparing for salah

'**Islam** requires **Muslims** to pray five times every day.

'Before we say **salah** we prepare ourselves. In order to focus our hearts and minds on **Allah**, before prayer we wash. This is called **wudu**. Wudu is compulsory and we can not make our salah without first making our wudu.

'Wudu, like salah, is written in the **Qur'an**. It requires the washing of different parts of our bodies, even if we are not very dirty.'

Imam Aurangzeb Khan

A Muslim performing wudu

Before washing for salah, Muslims get themselves into a prayerful frame of mind. The wudu always follows a set pattern:

- the hands are washed up to the wrists three times
- the mouth is rinsed three times
- the nostrils are washed three times, as is the tip of the nose
- the face is washed thoroughly three times
- both arms are washed up to the elbow three times
- wet hands are then passed over the hair from the forehead to the neck
- wet hands are run over the ears and neck
- both feet are washed up to the ankles.

As well as their daily salah, Muslims can also make their own private and personal prayers at any time. This type of prayer is called **du'a**. Du'a allows every Muslim to tell Allah about their own concerns: for example, to pray for someone who is ill. Du'a also provides a chance to think about the wonderful gifts Allah has given.

Du'a prayer

Different types of prayers can be included in du'a. These may include:

- adoration – praising Allah
- intercession – praying for the needs of others
- supplication – asking for the strength to overcome the pressures of the world and to grow in **faith**
- confession – saying sorry before Allah for doing wrong.

Set prayers at salah

Set prayers are repeated at salah, with each of the different positions which make up a **rak'ah**. It is very important for Muslims to follow the correct procedure. These are some of the prayers which Muslims say at salah.

'Allah is the greatest.'

'O Allah, glory and praise are for you, and blessed is your name, and exalted is your majesty: you alone are God.'

'I seek shelter in Allah from **Shaytan**.'

'In the name of Allah, the most merciful, the most kind.'

'Glory to you my Lord, the great.'

'Allah hears those who praise him.'

'Praise to you, our Lord.'

'Glory to you my Lord, the highest.'

'Peace and mercy of Allah be upon you.'

The opening chapter of the **Qur'an** is always recited during salah, and a further passage is also selected and read out.

Worship – Sawm

In this section you will:

- find out about the importance of fasting in the lives of Muslims
- consider the ways in which fasting can strengthen people
- read about worship during Ramadan.

Sawm

Sawm is the fourth pillar of **Islam.** Sawm means 'fasting' (going without food or water) from dawn to sunset every day during the month of **Ramadan**. Travellers and those who are ill during Ramadan can put off not eating and drinking and make up for it later.

Sawm develops self-control. It is also an opportunity for **Muslims** to refresh their hearts and minds in their worship of **Allah**.

By fasting, Muslims feel what it is like to be hungry. This helps them to feel for all the poor and hungry people in the world. Fasting teaches Muslims to control the love of comfort and to control sexual desires. The **Qur'an** is clear that eating, comfort and sex are three things which must be kept under control in order to live as Allah's servants.

'O you who believe! Fasting is prescribed for you as it was prescribed for those before you that you may become pious.'

Qur'an, **surah** 2: 183

A Muslim family breaking the fast at the end of Ramadan

Fasting then, is a sign of a truly obedient Muslim. The following actions will break the fast:

1. eating or drinking
2. anything going into the body through the nose or mouth; this includes smoking
3. having any sexual relations.

Muslims are also expected to make an extra effort not to tell lies, break a promise or do anything deceitful.

The importance of sawm

The main reason for fasting is to make a Muslim able to control passions and desires so that they become people of good deeds and intentions. At the end of Ramadan Muslims celebrate with a day of celebrations. The festival of **Id-ul- Fitr** is one of the great occasions for the Muslim community. On this day, Muslims offer special prayers at the **mosque** and thank Allah for all that he has given.

As well as fasting in Ramadan, Muslims can fast during other times of the year. This extra fasting helps them refocus their hearts and minds on Allah and increase their awareness of the needs of others.

Not fasting

Although most Muslims can and will take part in fasting during Ramadan, sometimes it is not possible for a person to fast.

Very young children and the elderly are not expected to fast at all, and neither are women who are pregnant. If a Muslim is ill or is travelling during Ramadan, they are excused from fasting at that time, but are expected to make up for any missed days later.

Worship during Ramadan

The month of Ramadan is very important to Muslims. It is the month in which the Qur'an was first revealed to the **prophet Muhammad** (**pbuh**).

During the month of Ramadan there is one night which to Muslims is 'better than a thousand months' (Qur'an, surah 97: 3). This night is called Lailatul Qadr (the Night of Power) and it falls, according to the Hadiths, during the last ten days of the month. Many Muslims will pass this night in worship for as long as they can.

During the month of Ramadan extra prayers are said and extra efforts made during salah. Tarawih is a special prayer in which Muslims attempt to read out as much of the Qur'an as possible. In many mosques, the whole of the Qur'an is read out through Tarawih prayer. Although usually said by the congregation at the mosque, any Muslim who can not attend the mosque should try to say Tarawih at home.

The mosque

In this section you will:

- find out about the Muslim place of worship
- reflect upon the variety of ways in which the mosque is used by Muslims.

The importance of the mosque

Most **Muslim** communities have a special building set aside for worship. These buildings are called **mosques**. Mosques are important as they serve the local people in a number of ways.

The main features of a mosque will include:

- the main prayer hall
- a separate section for women
- a domed ceiling, a symbol of the heavens above
- a **minaret**, a tower from which the people are called to prayer five times each day
- a **minbar**, a raised platform
- a **mihrab**, an archway showing the exact direction of Makkah.

Mosques also have running water and separate rooms for women and men to place their shoes and to complete their **wudu**.

Mosques will often include offices and a number of rooms used for a variety of community needs, including:

- the mosque school where Muslim children can learn Arabic and more about their **faith** (the **madrasah**)
- rooms for celebrations and parties
- courts to hear cases relating to Islamic law.

Prayers are said five times every day at the mosque and are lead by the **imam**. At the main Friday prayers, the imam will speak to the congregation from the minbar and give talks explaining the meaning of the Hadiths – the sayings of the prophet Muhammad (pbuh) – or the **surahs** (chapters) of the **Qur'an**.

A mosque in Jeddah, Saudi Arabia

'The mosque is used regularly, every day, for people to go and pray to Allah and to learn new things, every day of your life. I have spent time at the mosque madrasah, for seven years, I started when I was four, and finished when I was ten.'

Shamira, aged 13

'The most important prayers at the mosque are the Friday lunchtime prayers. I think Friday is important as it shows **Islam** is separate from other religions, Judaism has Saturday and Christianity Sunday.'

Mudassir, aged 15

Inside the Niujie mosque, the oldest mosque in Beijing, China

Beautiful mosques

The mosque is the place where Muslims meet to pray to Allah. Mosques are usually beautifully decorated. They may have richly coloured and patterned carpets and tiles, detailed stonework and chandeliers. The art and decorations which Muslims use are quite special.

Muhammad (pbuh) told his friends not to draw pictures of animals or people. He said that only Allah can make living beings, and it is wrong for human beings to try to imitate this. Muhammad (pbuh) was also afraid that if people were to pictures or statues they might begin to worship them. This would be idol worship. Idol worship is wrong because the Qur'an teaches that Muslims should only worship Allah.

Calligraphy

Muslim artists often draw beautiful flowers and plants. A highly developed art form in Islam, however, is calligraphy – the art of beautiful handwriting.

Calligraphy is often used to write out passages from the Qur'an. To write out the surahs in this way honours the words of Allah and is a wonderful privilege for the artist writing them.

Calligraphy is also used to create beautiful pictures, made up of letters, words from the Qur'an and prayers. It can be used on pottery and tiles, as well as on paper. It is in this way that all mosques have been decorated by Muslims to the glory of Allah over the centuries.

Holy books – the Qur'an

In this section you will:

- find out about the importance of the Qur'an for Muslims
- read some words from the Qur'an.

The Qu'ran: the word of Allah

Islam teaches that human beings are Allah's servants. This is a great responsibility and so **Muslims** believe that they need help to do their duty as Allah's servants. Muslims believe **Allah** alone is above all things. Therefore, He has sent **prophets** and messengers to show humans the right way to live. Allah has also given holy books for guidance.

'Allah's favours and blessings are countless. He provides us with all that we need. However, Allah's greatest favour is His guidance contained in the books of revelation. The pure, perfect and most useful knowledge comes only from Allah.'

Imam Aurangzeb Khan

The Qur'an – the word of Allah

The books of Allah

Muslims believe that Allah is behind the holy books mentioned in the **Qur'an**. These include the **Tawrah** (Torah) of **Musa** (Moses), the **Zabur** (Psalms) of **Dawud** (David), the **Injil** (Gospel) of '**Isa** (Jesus) and the Qur'an given to **Muhammad**. The Qur'an also mentions the **Sahifah of Ibrahim** (Scrolls of Abraham and Moses) (peace be upon them all).

Muslims believe that of all the holy books, only the Qur'an is in its original form. The Zabur, Tawrah and Injil have been gradually changed over the years. It is as though they have become a mixture of Allah's words with those of human beings. Islam teaches that the Qur'an is the most important of all Allah's revelations.

The message of the Qu'ran

'The message of the Qur'an is valid for all times and conditions. This is because the Qur'an contains the original messages revealed to Muhammad (**pbuh**). This message, passed from mouth to mouth and from heart to heart for over 1,400 years has enabled Muslims to know the true word of Allah.'

Imam Aurangzeb Khan

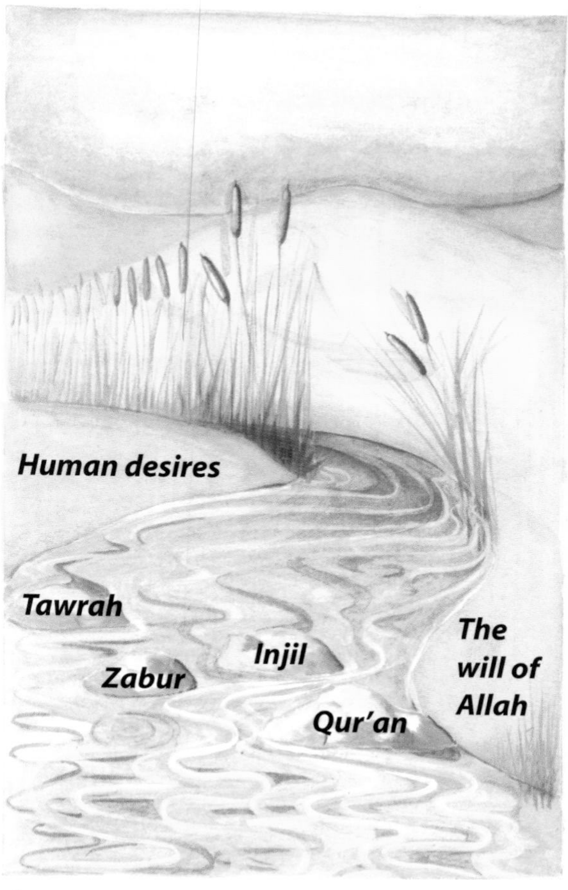

The way to Allah

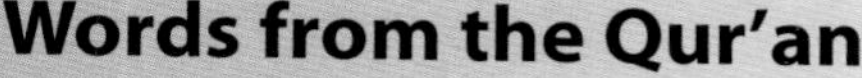

Words from the Qur'an

Here are some passages taken from the Muslim holy books.

'God chooses for Himself whoever He pleases, and guides to Himself those who turn (to Him).'

(surah 42: 13)

'O people of the Book, you have no ground to stand on unless you stand fast by the Law, the Gospel, and all the revelation that has come to you from God.'

(surah 5: 68)

'He will provide for you a light by which you will walk; He will forgive, for God always forgives and is most merciful.'

(surah 57: 28)

Respecting the Qur'an

Muslims treat the Qur'an with great respect. There are strict guidelines about how to do this.

The Qur'an is never allowed to touch the ground, and nothing should ever be placed on top of it. Before reading it, Muslims wash or bathe very carefully. They never handle the Qur'an without need. Whilst reading it, they do not speak, eat or drink. When they put it away, they keep it covered to protect it from dust.

Holy books – Hadiths

In this section you will:

- learn about how Muslims use the Hadiths
- understand the importance of Muhammad (pbuh) as an example to Muslims.

The importance of the Hadiths

Hadiths are important to **Muslims**. They are a collection of the words and teachings of the **prophet Muhammad** (**pbuh**). Muslims use them as a guide in their lives. This means that when they are faced with a difficult decision, a Muslim can seek the help of **Allah** through the words of the prophet Muhammad (pbuh).

'No Muslim can underestimate the importance and significance of the Prophet, it was through him that Allah chose to finally reveal Himself both in the words of the Qur'an and in the divine messages revealed though the Hadiths.'

Imam Aurangzeb Khan

Hadiths are used by Muslims to help them to live good lives. They provide guidance for living and can be used in a wide range of situations.

Examples of Hadiths

1. 'The best house … is the house in which an orphan is well treated and the worst house … is the house in which an orphan is badly treated.'

   'One who tries to help the widow and the poor is like a fighter for the way of Allah.'

2. 'Give me six things and I shall guarantee you paradise. When you speak, speak the truth, keep your

Muslims discussing the Hadiths

Two 'brother' Muslims

promise, be trustworthy, guard your chastity and lower your gaze and don't be arrogant.'

'Truth leads to virtue, and virtue leads to paradise.'

3 'Do not quarrel with your brother Muslim, don't make fun of him nor make him a promise which you cannot keep.'

'Each of you is a mirror of his brother, if you see something wrong in your brother, you must tell him to get rid of it.'

'None of you can be a believer unless he loves for his brother what he loves for himself.'

'A Muslim is he from whose words and deeds other Muslims are safe.'

4 'Every good action is love and it is a good action to meet a friend with a smiling face.'

'There is a man who gives charity and he conceals it so much that his left hand does not know what his right hand spends.'

Understanding the Word of Allah

The teachings that Muslims follow have been revealed either through the **Qur'an** or through the Hadiths which were given to the prophet Muhammad (pbuh). Muslims believe that Allah has shown His will through these teachings.

However, the question may be asked how reliable this revelation is, because it is human beings who have spread the message and written it down. In other words, what does it mean to talk of Allah's word as 'true'?

Fundamentalist scholars are so sure of the faith and trust that they have in Allah that they say that every word of the Qur'an and the Hadiths are true – word for word. They believe that they are the direct words of Allah. Even though they have been written down by human beings, fundamentalists believe that they have never been changed.

Liberal scholars view the written words of Allah as true. However, rather than being true word for word, they see them as being true in the way in which poetry is true. Poetry is full of imagery and symbol, myth and metaphor, and so is true at different times for those who write it and for those who read it.

The absolute truth of the revelations of Allah are fundamental to the **faith** of **Islam**.

Celebrating festivals

In this section you will:

- find out about the great Muslim festivals of Id-ul-Fitr and Id-ul-Adha
- think about how celebrating these festivals strengthens faith.

Muslim festivals

There are two great festivals in **Islam**. The first is **Id-ul-Fitr** at the end of **Ramadan**. The second is **Id-ul-Adha** which falls during the month of **Hajj**. The month of Hajj is the time of the pilgrimage to **Makkah**. Both festivals are a time for **Muslims** to give thanks to **Allah** for all he has given.

Both festivals involve worship and care for others. The whole family (**ummah**) of Islam feels very close during festival times.

Muslims prepare for their festivals in a number of ways:

- cleanliness: baths are taken and clean or new clothes worn
- prayer: Muslims come together in huge gatherings, to be as one
- thought for one's own family: presents are given, especially to children, special meals are eaten
- thought for others: **zakah** is collected and sent off.

After visiting the **mosque** on feast days, Muslims often go home by a different route. This is to create the best chance for meeting other Muslims, and spreading joy.

Id-ul-Fitr

Id-ul-Fitr celebrates the end of Ramadan, the month of fasting. The festival begins at the sight of the new moon. The new moon is the start of the new month. Muslims celebrate by decorating their houses. They give and receive cards and gifts. They go to the mosque for special prayers.

Zakah for Id-ul-Fitr is a special payment, the cost of two meals. This is given to the poor on behalf of each member of the family.

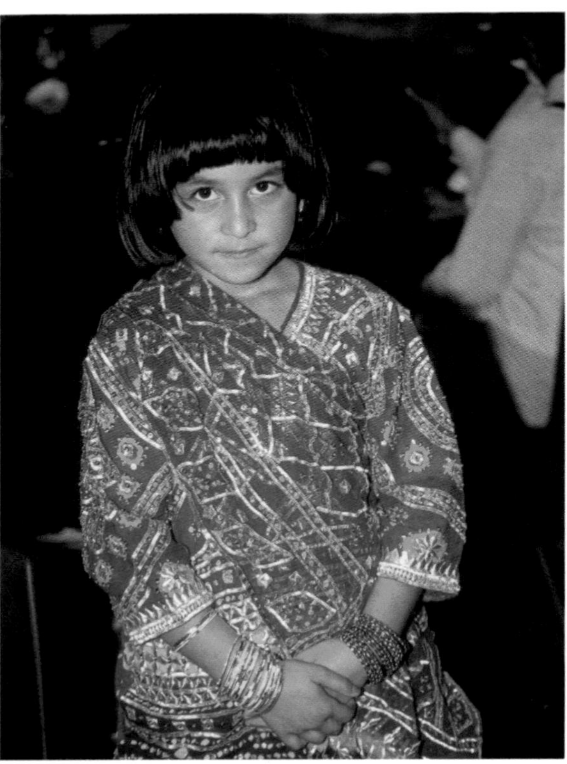

A Muslim dressed for Id

Id-ul-Adha

Id-ul-Adha is important for two reasons. Firstly, it is the end of the Hajj, the pilgrimage to Makkah. Secondly, it remembers the **faith** of the **prophet Ibrahim** (**pbuh**) when commanded to sacrifice his son **Isma'il** (pbuh).

Cards and gifts are given and received. But the most important feature of the festival is the sacrifice of an animal to Allah. The sacrifice remembers the ram that Allah provided for Ibrahim (pbuh) to sacrifice. This meant that he would not have to kill his son Isma'il (pbuh).

Muslims may sacrifice a sheep, goat, cow or camel. Muslim families enjoy a big meal using the meat from their sacrifice. They share the rest of the meat with the poor or with friends and relatives.

Celebrating in the love of Allah

The Muslim festivals

Each month in the Muslim calendar follows the lunar cycle, and is 29–30 days long. Because of this, Muslim festivals fall on different dates in the Western calendar.

These are the dates of the most important Muslim festivals.

1 Muharram: the Day of Hijra (the Muslim New Year, which remembers Muhammad's (pbuh) journey from Makkah to **Madinah**)

10 Safar: Ashura

12 Rabi ul-Awwal: Maulid ul-Nabi (Muhammad's (pbuh) birthday)

27 Rajab: Isra' wal Mir'aj (Muhammad's (pbuh) night journey, when he was taken to heaven)

27 Ramadan: Lailat-ul-Qadr (the Night of Power, when Muhammad (pbuh) began to receive the Qur'an)

1 Shawwal: Id-ul-Fitr (celebrates the end of the month of fasting)

10 Dhul Hijja: Id-ul-Adha (remembers the story of Ibrahim (pbuh) and Isma'il (pbuh))

'I enjoy celebrating Id because it's thanking Allah for the family and friends we have and sharing a happy time with them.'

Shamira, aged 13

Pilgrimage – Hajj 1

In this section you will:

- learn about why Muslims go on pilgrimage to Makkah
- understand the importance of entering the state of ihram
- read about the two main groups of Muslims today.

Pilgrimage to Makkah

Hajj is the fifth pillar of **Islam**. It is a pilgrimage to **Makkah**. A pilgrimage is a journey made to a place special to your religion. **Muslims** are to go on Hajj at least once in a lifetime, if they can afford it.

When Muslims pray, they face Makkah. In fact they face the **Ka'bah**, the House of **Allah**. It was the first place built for the worship of Allah. Muslims believe that Allah has made the Ka'bah holy. Every year, Muslims come from all over the world to join fellow Muslims in worship in Allah's House.

During Hajj, the Islamic community (the **ummah**) is very strong. Barriers of language and race disappear as all worship together. Everyone is equal in the House of Allah – they are all His servants.

'It was the most amazing moment of my life. Standing before God at the foot of Mount Mercy with 2,000,000 of my fellow

The Ka'bah

Muslims really did bring my **faith** alive for me. I have always tried hard to keep the teachings of the **Qur'an**, and live my life as a good person, but this was different. Everything that I have ever been taught, the events in the life of the Prophet that I had only heard about, was real. To bear witness with so many others is an experience that I shall never forget.'

Mamood, aged 24 – **Hajji**

Muslims in ihram

Ihram

While approaching Makkah before the Hajj begins, pilgrims must put on **ihram**. For men, ihram consists of two sheets of unsewn white cloth. This is a very simple form of dress which male pilgrims must wear in place of everyday clothes. For a woman, ihram does not require special clothes, but they do have to dress simply and wear a veil covering their hair.

Ihram is very important. It reminds the pilgrim that they are a humble servant of Allah. While in the state of ihram, pilgrims must not:

- use perfume
- kill or harm animals, even insects
- break or uproot plants
- do anything dishonest or arrogant
- carry weapons
- cover the head (males)
- cover the face (females)
- cut hair
- clip nails
- have sexual relations.

United before Allah

Hajj brings together Muslims from all around the world. It also brings together Muslims from the two main groups within Islam – Sunni Muslims and Shi'ah Muslims.

After the death of **Muhammad** (**pbuh**) there were arguments as to who should lead the Muslims. Those who supported the **prophet's** descendants became known as the 'Shiat Ali', or the Party of Ali. They are now called Shi'ites. They claimed that Ali was really the first true leader after Muhammad (pbuh).

Sunni Muslims see themselves as the true followers of Muhammad (pbuh). They believe that Muhammad (pbuh) had planned to have elections so that the best man would succeed as leader.

Sunnis are the largest group in Islam, with 90 per cent of all Muslims belonging to this group. The Shi'ites, on the other hand, make up only 10 per cent of modern Muslims.

Pilgrimage – Hajj 2

In this section you will:

- find out about the duties performed by Muslims on Hajj
- learn about requirements Muslims should meet to perform the Hajj
- read about the story of Ibrahim (pbuh) and Isma'il (pbuh).

The duties of Hajj

Muslims performing **Hajj** can be described as one equal family before **Allah**. It is as one family that the duties of Hajj are carried out.

- Pilgrims walk around the **Ka'bah** seven times.
- They then run between the hills of **Safa** and **Marwah**. This is where **Hajar** looked for water for her child. Allah gave them the Well of Zamzam. Pilgrims still stop to drink the water.
- Pilgrims then travel out of **Makkah** along the plain of **Arafat**. Two million pilgrims camp here.
- Pilgrims stand together on Mount Arafat (The Mount of Mercy). It is an opportunity to promise to love Allah and to follow his laws.
- The camp then moves on to Muzdalifah, between Arafat and Makkah. Pilgrims collect small stones to throw at the pillars at **Mina**.
- At Mina, pilgrims throw stones at three stone pillars that represent the devil. This symbolizes a rejection of the devil.
- Pilgrims then camp at Mina for two days for the Feast of Sacrifice (**Id-ul Adha**). An animal is sacrificed in thanksgiving for the ram Allah gave to **Ibrahim** (pbuh).

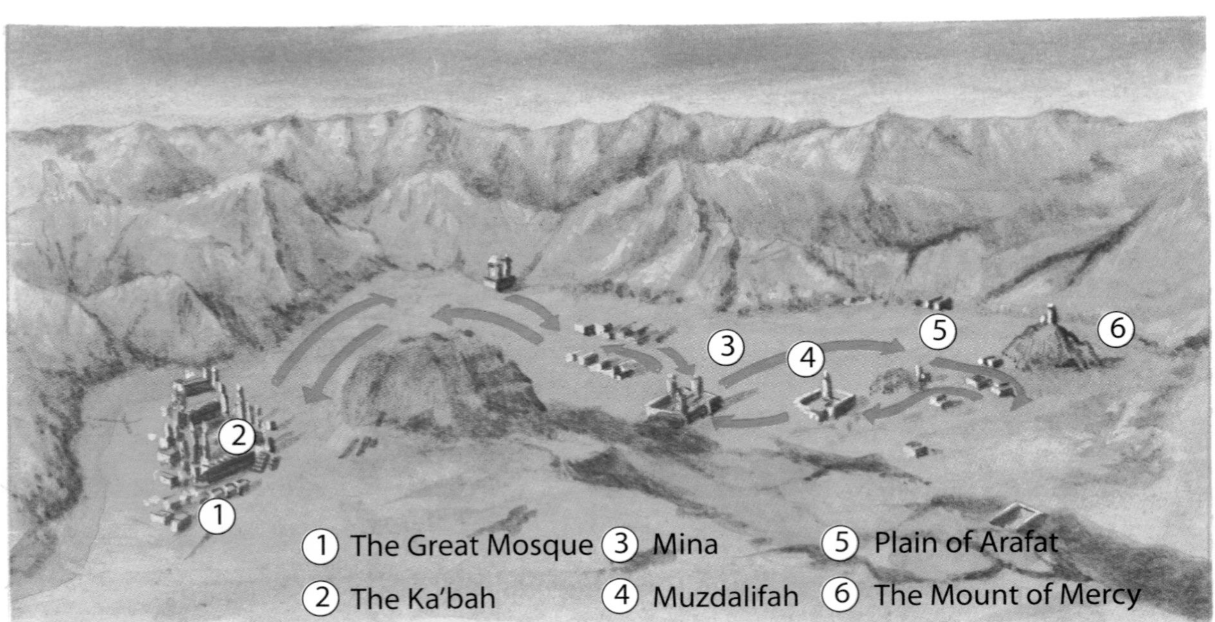

The route of the Hajj

- As an outward sign of the completion of Hajj, men will have their heads shaved (unfurling) and women will cut at least 2.5cm from their hair.
- Pilgrims will then return to Makkah to circle the Ka'bah again before going home.

Male Muslims who have performed Hajj take the name **Hajji** and women **Hajjah**. This is a great honour for Muslims.

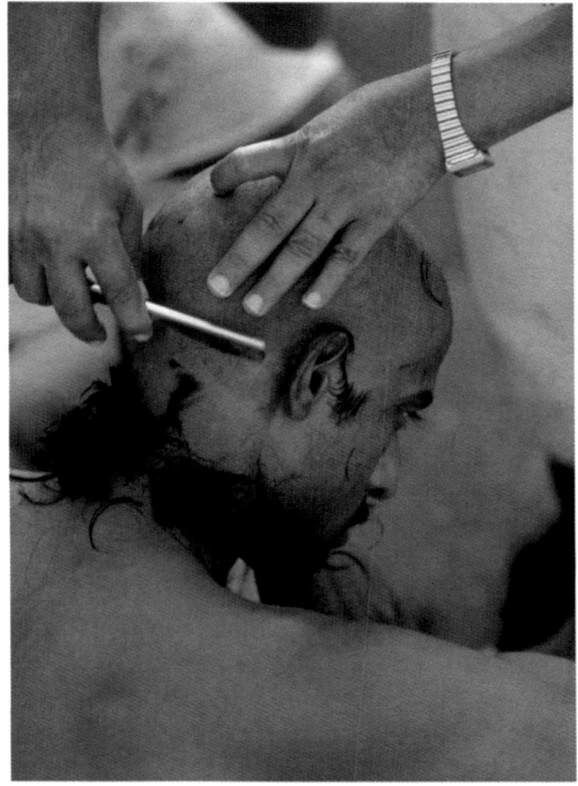

The unfurling

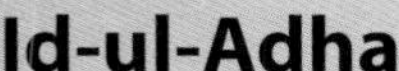

Id-ul-Adha

Id-ul-Adha remembers the story of Ibrahim (pbuh) told in the **Qur'an** – a story of complete **faith** and submission to Allah's will.

Ibrahim (pbuh) had made a promise to dedicate his life to the will of Allah. One night, Ibrahim (pbuh) had a dream in which he was asked to sacrifice his only son **Isma'il** (pbuh) to Allah. He was very upset, but he spoke to his son and they agreed to do what Ibrahim (pbuh) had been told to do.

They travelled to Mina, where the sacrifice was to take place. Isma'il (pbuh) lay face down on the altar, ready to be sacrificed. At the last moment, however, Allah stopped Ibrahim (pbuh) and gave him a ram to sacrifice in place of his son.

Rules for pilgrims

Muslims who perform Hajj must first meet certain requirements. First of all, they must be Muslims – non-Muslims are not permitted to take part in the pilgrimage. They must be physically and mentally fit, so that they can cope with and fully understand what they are doing. They must also have enough money to pay for their pilgrimage and to support any family members they leave behind during Hajj.

Rites of passage

In this section you will:

- discover the ways in which Muslims celebrate birth
- understand the importance of marriage to Muslims
- learn about aqiqah – the naming ceremony for babies.

Everyone enjoys a celebration. Having fun at a party or sharing a good time with family and friends is not difficult. The reasons for some celebrations are very important. The birth of a baby or two people getting married are important to both religious and non-religious people. This is a chance to find out something of the way in which **Muslims** mark these two special occasions. Such special occasions are often called rites of passage.

Birth

The birth of a baby is a reason for great joy. The new baby is welcomed into **Islam** as soon as it is born. The head of the family whispers the **adhan** (the call to prayer) into its ear. So the first word every Muslim baby hears is **Allah**. Prayers, usually led by the community's **imam**, are said for the baby and the family.

A newborn baby hearing the adhan for the first time

Marriage

Muhammad (**pbuh**) said:

'A woman should only be married to a person who is good enough for her or compatible to her.'

Hadith

For Muslims, the only sort of compatibility that really matters is **faith**. Muhammad allowed marriages between people of different social status and backgrounds. He knew that compatibility depended more on how much the couple loved Allah than anything else.

The secret of a successful Muslim marriage is shared values and **beliefs**. Even if the couple come from different cultures and backgrounds, hopefully they will have the same basic religious beliefs that will help to bind them ever closer together.

'Do not marry only for a person's looks, their beauty might become the cause of moral decline.'

'Do not marry for wealth, since this may become the cause of disobedience Marry rather on the grounds of religious devotion.'

Hadiths

A Muslim marriage

Islam teaches that marriage is the duty of every human being. Finding a good life partner and building a life together is very important.

The Muslim marriage service is a social ceremony. Because it is not a religious ceremony, it can take place anywhere licensed for marriages. The imam leads prayers asking for Allah's blessing for the couple and their families.

The choice of a marriage partner is often made by the parents. Sometimes they will look within the family, maybe a cousin. For many couples, love is expected to come after the marriage and not before.

Today, in some Muslim families customs are changing. Some people are happier finding their own partner. But there is still an expectation that partners will be suitable for each other in the eyes of their families as well.

Muslim names

Seven days after the birth of a Muslim baby comes the celebration of **aqiqah**. This is when the baby is named.

First of all, the baby's head is shaved, and by tradition the same weight as the hair in gold or silver is given to the poor. Even if the baby has no hair, a donation of money is still given. Some Muslims also offer a sacrifice to give thanks for the birth.

The choice of name is important. The name given is usually a family name or one of the names from the Muhammad's (pbuh) family.

For boys, some of the names often chosen start with '**Abd**', which means 'slave'. Abd will be added to one of the 99 different names for Allah, for example:

Abdullah (Servant of God)

Abdul Rahman (Slave of the Merciful)

Abdul Karim (Slave of the Generous One).

This shows that, whatever else they may do in life, first of all they must be a faithful servant of Allah.

Creation

In this section you will:

- find out what Muslims believe about the creation of the universe
- learn about the different beliefs about creation held by Muslims, Jews and Christians
- read about Islamic food laws.

The power of Allah

Most religions have a story that explains the creation of the world. The **Qur'an** is very clear about creation. It states that all things come from **Allah**. It is to Allah that all shall return when their time on earth is over.

'It is Allah who has created the heavens and the earth, and all that is between them in six days. Then he rose to his throne that suits his majesty. Mankind has no God besides Allah, as protector and helper. Remember this, Allah manages and regulates every thing on earth and in heaven and when everything has had its time it will return to him.

'Allah alone is the all-knower of the seen and unseen, the all-mighty, the most merciful. It was he who created all goodness and began the creation of Mankind from clay. Then he made offspring – male and female. Then he made all other living things upon earth.'

Qur'an, from **surahs** 21 and 32

Earth from space

At the completion of his creation, Allah said:

And the earth! We have spread it out, and set thereon mountains standing firm, and have produced therein every kind of lovely growth in pairs.'

Qur'an, surah 50: 7

The creation

Muslims believe that Allah created the whole universe. Allah created things in pairs so that creation may be perfectly balanced. Balance can be seen in the creation of the sky and the earth, the sea and dry land. Also there is balance in light and darkness, and male and female.

Like the Jewish Torah and Christian Bible, the Qur'an tells of creation in six days.

The Qur'an also mentions the creation of beings not mentioned in either the Torah or Bible.

Like Jews and Christians, Muslims believe that human beings were created from clay. But Muslims also believe that **angels** (slaves of Allah who always do what Allah wants) were created from light. They also believe that **jinn** (beings created with free will, living in a parallel world to our own) were created from fire. Of all that Allah has made, human beings are the most important.

The importance of humans is clear in this story. Allah brought all the angels and all the jinn before **Adam** (**pbuh**), the first man, and told them to bow down. This was because Adam was the most wonderful thing that Allah had ever created. All the angels and jinn bowed down. Only one jinn called **Shaytan** (the Devil) refused. As a punishment, Allah sent Shaytan away from his presence. In return, Shaytan promised to spend all his time and power tempting humans to sin.

Haram foods

Haram foods, which Muslims are not allowed to eat, include:

- any products made from a pig
- meat containing blood
- meat from an animal which dies due to disease or other natural causes
- any flesh-eating animal
- any animal that has been killed either by another animal or by any means made haram by Allah
- any animal that has been sacrificed to idols.

Food laws

Like many other religions, **Islam** teaches that some foods are allowed (**halal**) and some foods are not allowed (haram).

Muslims are allowed to eat all types of fruit, vegetables and grains. The main restrictions are to do with animal products. In order to be halal, an animal which is killed has to have all the blood in it drained away. **Islamic** law says that the animal should be killed by a sharp knife in the neck. Allah's name is repeated over the animal to show that the food is being taken with Allah's permission.

Meat of animals not killed in this way is regarded as haram. All parts of these animals are haram.

Muslims should buy halal meat from Muslim butchers, and should make sure that they do not eat haram food by mistake.

Environment

In this section you will:

- understand the Muslim belief that all creation is Allah's
- read about and reflect upon the Muslim belief that Allah has placed humans on earth to act as stewards to His creation.

A tropical rainforest

Allah's gift of creation

Muslims believe that **Allah** wants humans to look after this planet. The **Qur'an** teaches that human beings have been created by Allah and put on earth as stewards (**khalifah**), to take responsibility for all of Allah's creation. Muslims are commanded to make careful use of resources such as water. They are to respect animals and to replace any natural resources used wherever possible.

'It is He who has made you custodians, inheritors of the Earth.'

Qur'an, **surah** 6: 165

Care for all creatures

Muslims expect to be judged by Allah on how well they look after creation. This includes all creatures and all the natural resources that Allah has given.

Many Muslims are concerned with the well-being of creatures. Allah has given some animals as food. But **Muhammad** (**pbuh**) banned any 'sport' which involved making animals fight one another. So **Islam** condemns modern blood sports such as fox hunting. Islam teaches that no one should ever hunt just for fun.

'If someone kills a sparrow for sport, the sparrow will cry out on the Day of Judgement, "O Lord! That person killed me for nothing! He did not kill me for any useful purpose!"'

Hadith

Respecting all that Allah has created

All hunting should be for food. Any animal used for hunting should be well-trained and kept under control.

Experiments are carried out on animals for many reasons. Some of these are medical, others are for cosmetic purposes. Muslims believe that any experiment just for the development of luxury goods is wrong. Muslims should always find out if the things they buy have been produced using **halal** (permitted by Allah) methods.

Medical experiments are different. If there were no alternative to an experiment on an animal, then Muslims might accept it. But they would prefer to look for some other method that didn't hurt animals.

'Allah it is He who has subjected…to you all that is in the Heavens and all that is in the Earth.'

Qur'an, surah 45: 12–13

Human responsibility

Muslims believe that Allah has given people free will. This means that we are free to decide how we treat the planet we live on. Islam teaches that this planet is a place created out of the love of Allah. So we should look after it through love.

Islam teaches that Muslims should try to live at peace with nature.

The Assisi Declaration 1986

In 1986 Muslims met with members of all the major world religions in Assisi. They met to discuss how, as people of **faith**, they could suggest ways of looking after the world for the use and enjoyment of future generations.

The place and timing of the meeting was no accident. Assisi was the home of a man called St Francis. Although a Christian, St Francis has been accepted by many people as someone who had a particular love for nature and cared for it deeply. 1986 was the 25th anniversary of the World Wide Fund for Nature, an organization set up to look after the earth's natural environment.

All the different faiths made statements about 'religion and nature'. Muslims declared: 'Allah's people are responsible for the unity of His creation, its wildlife and natural environment… Unity cannot be had by setting one need against another or one end over another; it is maintained by balance and harmony.'

Abuses of Allah's creation

In this section you will:

- understand creation as Allah's gift to humanity
- consider the ways in which people abuse Allah's gift
- think about how humans can live with respect.

The **Qur'an** teaches that people have been placed on earth to act as **Allah's** stewards (**khalifah**). This means they must look after Allah's creation. But many people do not always do a very good job. People abuse Allah's creation in many different ways.

The planet

One abuse of Allah's creation is the way in which the rainforests are being cut down. It is true that timber is needed, but Allah has provided the rainforests for a special reason. Carbon dioxide is a gas produced when something is burned. This gas is turned into oxygen by trees. The more trees, the more oxygen, but fewer trees mean more carbon dioxide in the atmosphere.

Ourselves

Another concern for **Muslims** is alcohol. Alcohol is strictly forbidden in **Islam**. The reason for this is that alcohol can cause people to lose control. A famous story told by Muslims shows this to be true.

Destroying the rainforest

Muhammad (pbuh) spoke out against the use of alcohol

'Alcohol is the key to all evils. A man was brought and asked either to tear the Holy Qur'an, or kill a child, or bow in worship to an idol, or drink alcohol, or sleep with a woman. He thought the less sinful thing was to drink the alcohol, so he drank it. Then he slept with the woman, killed the child, tore the Holy Qur'an and bowed in worship of the idol.'

A Muslim tale

Islam teaches that **Shaytan** uses different ways to turn people away from belief in Allah, and alcohol is just one.

At the time of **Muhammad** (**pbuh**), many people enjoyed drinking alcohol. The teaching of Allah in the Qur'an accepted human weakness, and the prohibition of alcohol was given in stages.

As the news spread through Madinah, the effect was amazing. People even poured away the drinks they held in their hands. They smashed their wine bottles and poured the liquid away. From that time few, if any, true Muslims have ever drunk alcohol.

Living with respect

We as human beings are but a small part of Allah's universe. However, Muslims believe that we are a very important part because Allah has put us here to look after His creation.

Many people would want to suggest that the best way to look after the country in which we live is to treat all those that live in our society with respect. Only by working together can we treat our environment with respect.

Britain is a multicultural society. This means that people from a variety of religions, nationalities and backgrounds live in Britain today. One hundred years ago, it may have easily been assumed that your neighbours would have been white, British-born and claim to be Christian. Today this is not the case. In 1991, more than 3 million people living in Britain were from ethnic groups other than white British. Living together with respect is a positive way to look after Allah's creation.

Human rights

In this section you will:

- learn about human rights
- understand the importance of basic human rights for Muslims.

Islam teaches that **Allah** has created everyone. **Muslims** believe that there are basic rights that are shared by all people. These rights should be for every society, even if the society is not Muslim.

Allah has given these human rights and it is the duty of Muslims to protect them. Muslims believe that human life is sacred – which means it is special to Allah. So all human beings should be treated with respect.

The earth has many resources. There is enough for everyone to live well. No human being should go hungry while others waste what they have. Islam teaches that suffering must be dealt with. The hungry should be fed. The naked should be clothed and the sick given medical treatment. This teaching applies to all people, whether Muslim or not.

*The **ummah** before Allah*

Sufferers of famine

Muslims believe that it is wrong to make fun of people. We may laugh with people, to share happiness, but we must never laugh at people.

Muslims believe that people should never be forced to act against their own will.

Muslims believe that no one should go to prison unless they are proved guilty of some crime. Justice is to be open and unbiased.

Muslims believe power is only given to human beings on trust from Allah. It is their duty to speak out against dictators. They should protect the weak from oppression. To Muslims, a dictator is a ruler who tries to force his own will on other people. All people should seek the will of Allah. Allah's will is always based on kindness and justice.

Protecting people's freedom

It is the duty of an Islamic state to promote right and forbid wrong (**Qur'an**, **surah** 22: 44).

According to the Qur'an, the state should look after all its citizens – Muslims and non-Muslims alike. All citizens should enjoy freedom of belief, thought, conscience and speech. Every citizen should be free to develop their potential and earn a living wage. All citizens should enjoy the right to speak out on issues they consider right or wrong, remembering that the Islamic state should always try to implement the laws of the Qur'an.

A Muslim state should ensure a fair share of wealth. Islam does not believe in equal shares because this is against the law of creation. Allah requires fairness, not equality, for all.

Some Muslims are sad that there is not a single perfect Islamic state in the world today. It is true that there are many Muslim countries. Many feel that a true Islamic state should be based on the model of the **prophet Muhammad's** (**pbuh**) state in Madinah. However, organized efforts are being made in many parts of the world to bring about total change in society by setting up an Islamic system of government to follow the laws of the Qur'an fully.

Caring for others – Zakah

In this section you will:

- learn about zakah, the third pillar of Islam
- think about how zakah can make a difference to the lives of all Muslims
- read about how Muslims treat money.

A Muslim making a zakah contribution

Caring for others

All **Muslims** are expected to be charitable and to care for the wider community. For example, a baker's shop could give away what it had left on a Thursday night. This would mean that no one nearby need say his or her Friday prayers hungry. Also, a Muslim could send money to support an appeal or disaster fund.

The **prophet Muhammad** (**pbuh**) encouraged giving:

'He who eats and drinks while his brother goes hungry, is not one of us.'

Hadith

Zakah

In addition to acts of charity, Muslims are expected to share their income and wealth. This is one of the duties of all Muslims. They hand over a certain amount each year to support those who are poor in the community. This is not a matter of choice, but a religious duty. This duty is called **zakah**. Zakah is the third pillar of **Islam**.

Muslims do not see zakah as a charity or a tax. Charity is optional and taxes can be used by the state for any purpose. Zakah has to be spent for purposes such as helping the poor and needy. It is also used to help those in debt and travellers in need. Zakah is really an act of worship. Muslims pay zakah to please **Allah**. Zakah gives Muslims the opportunity of sharing wealth with those less fortunate.

Helping the poor

Rates of zakah

Wealth	Amount	Rate
Cash in hand or bank	Over the value of 595g of silver	2.5%
Gold and silver	85g of gold or 595g of silver	2.5%
Trading goods	To the value of 595g of silver	2.5%
Cows	30	1
Goats and sheep	40	1
Mining produce	Any	20%
Agricultural produce	Per harvest: Rain-watered land Irrigated	 10% 5%

Muslims see all wealth as really belonging to Allah. He is seen as the real owner and people are just looking after his wealth. Through the payment of zakah, the rich share their wealth with the poor. This provides a fair share of Allah's riches for all.

A duty of care

Islam is a way of life. Muslims are more than just a group of believers. They have a duty of care for each other in the name of Allah. The way in which Muslims deal with earning and sharing wealth reflects this point well.

Muslims argue that wealth and resources should be shared more equally between people throughout the world.

The Muslim economic system

Islamic laws rule the ways in which Muslims can earn and spend their money. As well as the duty to make zakah contributions, Muslims may not:

- earn money from the production or sale of alcoholic drinks, from gambling and lotteries
- earn money by illegal means, such as theft, deceit, fraud and so on
- earn money through any business which involves charging interest, which Islam teaches is a means of exploitation.

Muslims see the modern 'free market economy' as against the most basic of Allah's wishes for humankind – that fairness and justice should be available to all. Islam teaches that a system of zakah is more just.

Women in Islam

In this section you will:

- find out about what the Qur'an teaches about the status of women in Islam
- think about issues relating to modern Muslim women
- read about women and Allah.

Women have a very important place in the **Muslim** community. Once, a person asked **Muhammad** (**pbuh**), 'Who deserves the best care from me?' The **prophet** replied, 'Your mother, then your mother then your mother then your father and then your nearest relatives.'

'O people, your wives have certain rights over you and you have certain rights over them.'

The prophet also said:

'The best amongst you is the one who is best towards his wife.'

Hadiths

These sayings show the important place that should be given to women in **Islam.**

However, there are some people who have doubts about the status of women in Islam. Some people feel that a Muslim woman is almost a prisoner in her own house, someone who has no rights and is living under the domination of men.

A group of Muslim women

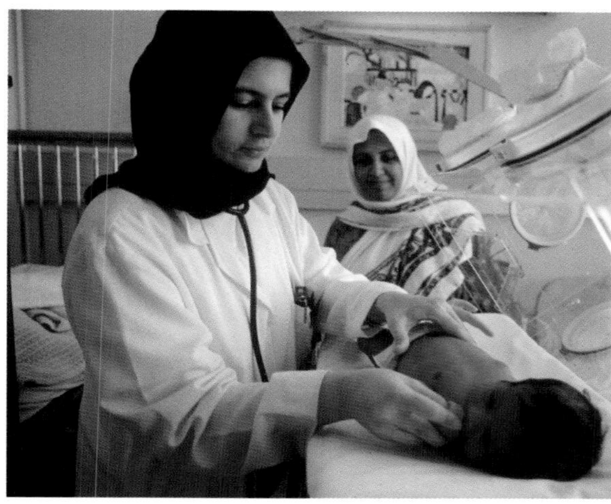

A Muslim woman at work

Muslims believe that **Allah** has created all living creatures in pairs, male and female. This includes humankind. Islam teaches that Allah has blessed both males and females. So Muslim women have certain rights and responsibilities: for example, the right to choose their husband. No one can make a woman marry against her will. She also has a right to seek a divorce from her husband if their marriage breaks up.

A woman has a right to develop her talents and to work. Also, non-Muslim women with Muslim husbands are expected to keep and practise their religion. The husband cannot interfere with this freedom.

It is the duty of the Muslim mother to bring up children according to Islam. She will usually look after the family and control domestic affairs. Muslim women should dress modestly, as should Muslim men. In some Muslim countries, women put on **hijab** (a covering cloak) while going out and meeting adult males other than close relatives.

Women and Allah

It is clear in this passage from the **Qur'an** that Muslim women are important in the sight of Allah. They were created by and are loved by Allah.

The Muslims, men and women,

the believers men and women,

the men and women who are obedient,

the men and women who are truthful,

the men and women who are patient,

the men and women who are humble,

the men and women who give Sadaqah,

(Zakah and alms to the poor)

the men and women who observe Sawm,

(Fasting during Ramadan)

the men and women who guard their chastity

and the men and women who remember Allah much with their hearts and tongues.

Allah has prepared for them forgiveness and a great reward (Paradise).

Matters of life and death

In this section you will:

- understand what is meant by the term 'human life is sacred' and apply Islamic teaching to issues surrounding abortion
- read about and reflect upon Islamic teaching regarding the afterlife.

Muslims believe that all human life is sacred, a gift of **Allah**.

'Do not kill anyone … killing Allah has forbidden.'

Qur'an, **surah** 17: 33

'It is He, Allah, Who makes laugh, and makes weep. It is Allah Who causes death and gives life. And that He Allah creates the pairs, male and female.'

Qur'an, surah 53: 42–5

Muslims believe that Allah has given every life an amount of time. No one knows when Allah will take it back. It is the duty of all Muslims to live every day as if it was their last. This means that they will be ready for the time when Allah will judge them.

'The knowledge of the Final Hour is with Allah; none can reveal the time but He. It shall not come upon you except all of a sudden.'

Qur'an, surah 7: 187

Islam teaches that death itself should never be feared.

'When their time comes, neither can they delay nor can they advance it an hour.'

Qur'an, surah 16: 61

Muslims should not fear death. This is because they do not believe it is the end of everything. They believe in the promise of an afterlife. This should, then, be a time of great joy as they will receive a reward for all their efforts on earth.

Muslims believe human life is one eternal life. Eternal life is made up of two parts, life before and life after death. Muslims believe that the spirit of life that Allah has given everyone survives death and enters the afterlife.

'Do you think that We shall not reassemble your bones? Yes, We are able to put together in perfect order the tips of fingers!'

Qur'an, surah 75: 3

Islam teaches that death is beyond human control. It is Allah alone who orders the hour of death.

A Muslim tombstone

Muslims are usually buried facing **Makkah**. It is best if they can have their own cemeteries, or their own special plot. This means that they may have their graves facing in the right direction.

As the body is lowered into the ground they say:

'In the name of God we commit you to the earth, according to the Way of the **Prophet** of God.'

A little earth is then thrown down with the words:

'We created you from it, and We return you into it, and from it We will raise you a second time.'

Qur'an, surah 20: 55

Money should not be spent on fancy tombstones, but donations given to the poor.

Mourning should not last for more than three days.

Last words

When death is very near for a Muslim, it is important for the person to be surrounded by family and friends. The person will ask their forgiveness and Allah's forgiveness for anything they have done wrong. If possible, the last words they say will be the **shahadah**, the declaration of **faith** in Allah.

A moral dilemma

Muslims believe that human life is sacred. However, should this make a difference to the way in which they think about other people?

The following situation is an example of a moral dilemma of the type that may face Muslims in Britain today, and the way in which they might respond to it.

An unmarried woman falls pregnant and is uncertain about how she feels. She is faced with a number of possibilities:

- to have the baby and bring it up
- to have the baby and put it up for adoption
- to have an abortion (an operation to end the pregnancy and remove the baby from the womb).

Islam teaches that all life is a gift from Allah and, as such, should be respected. Therefore, it appears at first that Muslims would be totally against abortion. However, Islam teaches that the spirit which makes a person who they are does not develop until the fourth month of pregnancy. This implies that, although not the ideal, an abortion would be allowed in certain circumstances.

Jihad

In this section you will:

- investigate the nature of jihad in Islam
- examine the reasons for the inclusion of jihad in the Muslim life of faith.

The nature of jihad

Jihad is Arabic for 'striving'. **Muslims** use the word jihad for any activity done for the love of **Allah**. Jihad requires Muslims to use all their energy to establish the Islamic way of life. Jihad is an on-going process for Muslims.

'The aim of jihad is to establish peace. At first we learn to control bad desires and intentions. Human beings must strive hard to achieve this.

Imam Aurangzeb Khan

Jihad demands the use of all material and mental resources. Muslims may sometimes be required to die for the cause of **Islam**.

The aim of jihad is to do the will of Allah. This is important because this is the basis of all Islamic practice. Jihad fits alongside the basic duties of **shahadah**, **salah**, **zakah**, **sawm** and **Hajj**. All these duties teach obedience to Allah. By fulfilling them, Muslims seek his blessing and hope to enter paradise, the place of joy and peace, when they die.

All Islamic duties should prepare Muslims for jihad. Jihad is at the heart of faith and the reason for salah, zakah, sawm and Hajj.

Muslim soldiers

'It is most important that we try hard to practise what we say.'

Imam Aurangzeb Khan

'Why do you ask of others the right conduct and you yourselves forget, have you no sense?'

Qur'an, **surah** 2: 44

The importance of jihad

'O you who believe! Why do you say that which you do not do? It is most hateful to Allah that you say that which you do not.'

Qur'an, surah 61: 2–3

These verses direct Muslims to put words into action. Muslims must carry out their duty to do good themselves and encourage others to do the same. This can include getting involved in charity work and organizations that help people in disaster areas, such as the Red Crescent (the Islamic version of the Red Cross).

A Red Crescent refugee camp

Jihad can also involve a violent struggle in order to establish the will of Allah. Violence is always tragic as Islam teaches that it is wrong unless absolutely necessary. Wherever possible, jihad is about changing hearts and minds by peaceful means rather than by force.

Prayers for peace

All of the major world religions teach that at the heart of God is peace. Therefore, they all have prayers for peace in a world torn apart by war. Here are three examples:

Lord make us instruments of your peace.
Where there is hatred, let us sow love,
Where there is injury, pardon,
Where there is doubt, faith,
Where there is despair, hope,
Where there is sadness, joy.

(Christianity)

Oh Allah, you are peace.
You are the source of peace.
You are full of blessings and sublime.

(Islam)

Cause us, our Father to lie down in peace,
And rise again to enjoy life.
Spread over us the covering of your peace,
Guide us with your good counsel
And save us for the sake of your name.

(Judaism)

Evil and suffering

In this section you will:

- think about what is meant by the problem of evil
- consider Muslim responses to the claim that Allah should stop evil and suffering
- read some prayers for peace.

Everyday the media brings us headlines about things often described as 'evil'.

Young family dies in house fire

Man convicted of murder

Earthquake kills thousands

Famine threatens Ethiopia

Leukaemia sufferer, 14, emergency bone marrow transplant essential

The effects of an earthquake

The problem of evil and suffering

Everyday people ask the question 'why?' Why, if there is an almighty God who has created all things out of love and compassion, do we suffer? Is it not impossible to believe in something all-powerful and all-loving that allows evil and suffering to exist? Either Allah is not all-powerful or else not all-loving, as evil and suffering do exist.

'I look at the sun, moon, sky, lakes and wonderful things like that that Allah can do. Then I look beyond these things, the wonderful things, and I see flooding, hurricanes and droughts. I ask myself, "How can Allah allow such things?"'

Anish, aged 13

Muslim responses

Muslims believe that Allah is indeed all-powerful and all-loving. It is for this reason has given all created things free will. Muslims would argue that it is the murderer who freely decides to take a life. Similarly, it is the free and natural course of things for earthquakes to occur.

Muslims believe that the will of Allah is beyond human understanding. In their prayers Muslims will often add 'If Allah wills'. This is because they know that all things are in Allah's hands and that they should trust Him.

'Or do you think that you shall enter Paradise without such trials as came to those who passed away before you?'

Qur'an, **surah** 2: 214

A personal reflection

There was once a young Muslim called Salim. One day when he was 13 years old his father told him some very sad news. Salim's mother had cancer, and she would not live for more than 5 or 6 months.

Salim was full of mixed emotion. He felt deep sorrow. He felt helpless, and he even felt guilty. Most of all, he felt angry – angry that Allah could allow such a thing to happen to his wonderful mother who, at 35, was far too young to die.

He prayed. He prayed for what seemed like hours every day telling Allah exactly how he felt. He was angry. Salim prayed that Allah would heal his mother and make her well.

His mother did not get well. She died following months of pain and distress. Salim was angry and could not understand how Allah could allow such a thing to happen.

Salim explained his feelings to his **imam**. The imam said that in a very real sense Salim's mother had been made well – she had been made whole again, and she now enjoyed the beauty and peace of paradise.

Although it still hurt not to have his mother with him, Salim understood what the imam meant. The life that Allah has given is more than just life on earth. It is eternal life.

The existence of Allah

In this section you will:

- understand the Muslim belief that the statement 'Allah exists' is a statement of fact
- think about arguments that have been put forward to prove Allah's existence
- read the story of a young Muslim called Salim.

Moved by the power of Allah

Faith and trust

Muslims proclaim their **faith** in the **shahadah**:

'Ash hadu an laa ilaha il-allahu wa Ash hada anna Muhammadar abduhu wa rasulu.'

(I believe there is no god but Allah; and I believe that **Muhammad** (**pbuh**) is the servant and messenger of Allah.)

For a Muslim to say 'I believe' shows they accept the reality of **Allah** in their hearts and minds.

'For all who profess the shahadah, Allah is as real as the beating of their own heart.'

Imam Aurangzeb Khan

Arguments for the existence of Allah

Some people who are not Muslims find the nature and existence of Allah difficult to understand and accept. For this reason, Muslim scholars have developed an argument to prove that Allah must exist.

The 'Kalam argument' states that:

- all things that exist have a cause
- it is impossible to go back forever looking for causes
- there must therefore have been a first cause, that was not caused itself
- Allah is the first cause as Allah is without cause.

The universe – the work of Allah

There are other possible arguments that could be put forward to demonstrate the fact of Allah's existence. For example, the fact that ever since the beginning of human history people have claimed to have experienced Allah shows the reality of Allah. How else would they have experienced Him?

Maybe the conditions for life on planet earth have been designed especially. If so, there must have been a designer. This designer must have been Allah, the only power capable of such things.

The very fact that human beings have an understanding of right and wrong must have come from somewhere. As children, we have all made mistakes and have been guided by our parents. They taught us the correct way to behave. It is argued that our understanding of right and wrong must have come from Allah. Muslims believe Allah to be the supreme law giver and moral guide of all.

The perfection of Allah

Muslims give Allah different 99 names. However, these 99 names can only scratch the surface of Allah's nature. One thing is clear, however: Muslims believe that Allah is perfect.

The fact that Islam teaches that Allah has all perfections can be used to argue that Allah must exist. To exist is perfection. Therefore, if Allah has all perfections, He must also possess the perfection of existence. Therefore, Allah must exist.

However, many would argue that existence is not a perfection, and here the argument falls. For Muslims, the success of this or any argument does not matter because the question of Allah's existence is simply a matter of faith and **trust**.

Glossary

Abd servant

Adhan the call to prayer

Akhirah belief in life after death

Allah God

Angel(s) messenger(s) from Allah, visible under certain conditions

Belief(s) firm opinion(s), acceptance without doubt

Blasphemy acting or speaking disrespectfully about Allah

Du'a personal prayer or supplication

Faith the courage to accept the challenges of belief

Hadith(s) sayings and traditions of Muhammad (pbuh)

Hajj annual pilgrimage to Makkah

Hajjah name given to a Muslim woman who has performed Hajj

Hajji name given to a Muslim man who has performed Hajj

Halal allowed

Hijab covering cloak worn by Muslim women

Ibadah worship, being a servant of God

Id-ul-Adha feast of sacrifice, ends the Hajj

Id-ul-Fitr feast to break the fast

Ihram state of religious 'separation' or purity

Imam a teacher or leader

Injil the revelation given to 'Isa (Jesus)

Islam submission to Allah

Istjfaa calling to prophethood

Jihad striving, holy war in defence of Allah's will

Jinn elemental spirit

Ka'bah the 'Cube', shrine of Allah in Makkah

Kalimah Tayyibah the last words spoken by a Muslim before dying

Khalifah deputy for Allah

Khutbah sermon

Madrasah school

Mihrab niche indicating the direction of Makkah

Minaret tower from which the call to prayer is given

Minbar pulpit for giving Friday sermons

Mosque place for communal prayer and activities

Muslims followers of Islam

Pbuh 'Peace be upon him' (said of the prophets)

Prophet(s) holy person (people), through who(m) Allah has revealed something of himself

Qur'an the Revealed Book

Ramadan the month of fasting

Risalah prophecy

Sahifah of Ibrahim scrolls of Abraham and Moses

Salah ritual prayer five times daily

Sawm fasting from sunrise to sunset

Shahadah declaration of faith

Shirk sin of associating anything with Allah

Surah(s) chapter(s) in the Qur'an

Tawhid the doctrine of the one-ness of Allah

Tawrah the revelation given to Musa (Moses) (pbuh)

Trust belief in the reliability or truth of something

Ummah the 'family' of Islam

Wudu ritual washing before prayer

Zabur the revelation given to Dawud (David) (pbuh)

Zakah giving of one-fortieth of savings for God's service

Places

Arafat Mount of Mercy, where Adam (pbuh) and Eve met after God forgave their sin

Jabal-un-Nur the Mountain of Light, where Muhammad (pbuh) regularly prayed in isolation in a cave

Makkah city of Ka'bah shrine, Muhammad's (pbuh) birthplace

Mina place of stoning the Devil on Hajj

Safa and **Marwah** places where Hajar searched for water

People

Abu Talib uncle of Muhammad (pbuh) who adopted him

Adam the first created man

Dawud the prophet David (pbuh), king of Israel

Hajar wife of Ibrahim (pbuh)

Ibrahim Abraham, the 'father' of Jews and Arabs, and 'friend of God'

'Isa the prophet Jesus, worshipped by Christians

Isma'il the prophet Ishmael, son of Abraham

Jibril (Gabriel) the angel who transmitted revelations to Muhammad (pbuh)

Khadijah first wife of Muhammad (pbuh)

Muhammad the last and greatest of the prophets, to whom Allah revealed the Qu'ran

Musa the prophet Moses

Shaytan Satan, the devil, the chief Jinn

Suleiman the prophet Solomon, son of Dawud (David) (pbuh)

Index